My Book of Colours and Shapes

Illustrated by Sharon Harmer

Miles
Kelly

Colours

Seven elves make a shoe.
Is it red or is it blue?

red

pink

purple

2

What colour are the shoelaces?

orange

yellow

blue

green

What is your favourite colour?

Red

A wolf is lurking in a wood,
He meets a girl in a red hood.

How many red apples can you count?

Ruby is a pinkish red named after the colour of the ruby gemstone

Do you have any red toys?

Yellow

Rapunzel gazes from her tower,
She longs to pick a golden flower.

Canary yellow is very bright – it is named after the canary bird

What colour is Old MacDonald's tractor?

What does Rumpelstiltskin spin straw into?

Blue

From the waves a mermaid spies
An icy sleigh in starry skies.

Turquoise is a greenish-blue colour

How many dolphins can you see?

What colour is the starfish?

Green

In the garden, lush and green,
Jack has found a magic bean.

Green is made
by mixing blue
and yellow

10

What colour is the door to the secret garden?

Orange

While at the tea table is sat
A hatter in an orange hat.

You make orange by mixing red and yellow

How many orange butterflies can you see?

Purple

At the party, fun on skates,
And purple cake on purple plates.

You make purple by mixing blue and red

What colour are the wizards' hats?

Pink

Dancing, prancing — would you think
Three pigs could turn even more pink?

You make pink by mixing red and white

How many fairies can you see?

13

Shapes

Painting faces slow and steady,
Do you think the teddy's ready?

How many red squares can you see?

triangle

square

circle

rectangle

What shape is the pink building block?

Circles

A circus show, a juggling clown,
A donkey gasps, "Can I lie down?"

A circle is round, with no corners

What shape is the wheel on the unicycle?

An oval is like a squashed circle

How many balloons can you see?

Squares and rectangles

Two sweet children need a treat —
This house looks good enough to eat.

A square has four sides of equal length, and four corners

What shape is the window of the gingerbread house?

How many lollipop trees can you see?

19

Triangles

A camping spot with trees to climb,
As Snow White calls, "It's picnic time!"

How many birds can you see?

A triangle has three sides

What shape is the witch's hat?

More than four sides

Through the windows stars shine bright,
Goodnight Beauty — do sleep tight.

star

How many stars can you see through the windows?

hexagon

pentagon

How many sides does a hexagon have?

Lots to spot

Sparkly jewels for you and me,
What would your three wishes be?

How many different colours and shapes can you name?